DEBTS & LESSONS

DEBTS & LESSONS

LYNN XU

OMNIDAWN PUBLISHING
RICHMOND, CALIFORNIA
2013

Cover art by Lynn Xu
"Study of Rousseau," 2012.

Cover design by Joshua Edwards
Interior layout by Cassandra Smith

Cataloguing-in-Publication Data is available from the Library of Congress.

Published by Omnidawn Publishing, Richmond, California
www.omnidawn.com   (510) 237-5472   (800) 792-4957
10 9 8 7 6 5 4 3 2 1
ISBN: 978-1-890650-80-3

For my mother and father

TABLE OF CONTENTS

SAY YOU WILL DIE FOR ME   9

OUR LOVE IS PURE   15

EARTH LIGHT   21

ENEMY OF THE ABSOLUTE   35

NIGHT FALLS   43

LULLABIES   55

D E B T S & ~~L E S S O N S~~   81

Language exists because nothing exists between those
who express themselves. All language is therefore
a language of prayer. Held in the dark, without sleep. Faith

is the confession that there exists that
wherein one is faithless. Wherein faith isolates a position of value there exists
two essential hells. The one you are in.

And the one you are after.
Sound is positioned in the other and is poetic because it is unspoken. *Incidence*
after *incidere* is positioned *in* from *cadere*, *to fall*. The point is incident

when it falls on the line is incident when it *passes through* a point even in the dark
is only an idealized limit of a smaller and smaller presence. The heart
which is an orgasm. A long dagger. The prayer exists

because it is positioned. In that presence
wherein the heart is expressed. Wherein sound is incident to the heart
exists. I am not asking you to die for me. Say you will die for me.

OUR LOVE IS PURE

I

Man

Makes love and love makes Rome. In Rome apart

From you

This autumn is a dream. I fell

Into the sea. Through the French trees. My heart

Became a suite in the Carlyle, compels you

To undress.

Foliage and cleavage sail like confetti onto our voyage.

II

Statues forgetting to crawl into death from the balconies

And battlefields. Love

From the battlefields. My blood went to breath

Like a younger poet, who made the dove

Crawl into a handkerchief. In the face of the poet, it's important to track

Which features are your own.

So age has brought lace from the sea onto your face.

Say past

These infrared trees, lay darkness sublime as stirred melodies.

III

Mind evaporates briefly twisting in

Little disappearances

Of meat. Fish

Meat everywhere mind is

Staring

Into your eyes.

Cloudless

Eyes. Ebi

Shinjo starry

Skies.

Friends to whom I belong. Friends whom I will wrong.

EARTH LIGHT

I

Doors open and shut.

We've come to the place where nothing shines.

I hear eternity

Is self-forgetting. Interiors warm with the nightmare of guests and poetry

And you. Everything darkly

Reverent years of reading about death eluded.

Bled

Back from the ear sidestepping your bullets bloom in on ye lay

Rock. Rud. Spread

So swiftly tastes like mud. Dredged mud off

The corpse sled hushed down woodsmoke.

Said the stars thrum on Marie

Marie. Hold on tight.

In the depths of outer space

Is man.

II

The blood that disappears

                    That is unsociable

                    Because of loss. I

                    Verboten.

                    I am you.

III

Back locked against the barrel there
Is the conscious world, greased, lay dead lands sir.
Lay dreadnaughts uncoupled on shoring brain dark in eelgrass slurred gristles stir
Ear and heel cross night crosses without pain.
To the west lay darkness.
Speak into it.
Spoked your thumb bade the tooth from its socket. Go on. Tear bones
From my desk
Lay
Your
Spoon
In
Cool
And Shakespearesque.

IV

Decay

Lets on a hum.

Listen.

I have to screw

A little thing

I have to screw. All is

Moved by love. Homer, the sea. All is not

To think

But dream of me.

V

Thumbed a loose rock in the sea
Blue with life. These pearls that were your eyes, tell
Me what you've seen, twinkling in the tea
Cups. Twisted back the shuttered sea, the eau
De cologne—how fast the black waters go.

VI

Let it not be for what you write, the world
I mean. And let us not return to death
Like students, the white rockets we have hurled.
Macbeth. Macbeth. Macbeth. Macbeth. Macbeth.
I muck my childish software to a church
On Madison Ave. Autumn summons bones
And careers. My breath to weekend its search.
I feel it in my bones. I swim with phones
Into the earth. My psychic says the sky
Is poetry. Is Niagara Falls.
And where our mothers wave and wave goodbye,
The witches have our pilot's thumb and calls.

VII

Each night a sweetness
Comes so tender
And sublime the devil
Turns his face into the soil.

VIII

Light. Hairy
Light how one
Laughs. Une
Obscénité. Un abîme.
Comme les ondes? Non. Dans l'ombre tu ôtes
Mon enfer à moi.

IX

Leveled your pistol lay on the current
Freckled with blood. I am not hell. Not dead.
The world has aged. Hell carried us, switched off
The blood. There, with no actual frontiers
To erase on the other side, the rough
Sound of the few leaves, the distant glitter.
The earth was all symbol. Turn your ghost that
Way such that I may mine, and with what.

X

Terror. The chocolate machine glistens
In the night. The universe hangs on this
Malheur. Mal de mer. The sea-worm listens
To its Latin noise, mingling parti pris
With the bastion of deal, its missing knob,
Terra infidel, how the lunar month
Makes appetite with its special eye. Slob
Jelly on eyelids slagged with salt. The month
Cannot end like this. And wanting nothing
Of this in mind the mind-englutted touch
Torches its prime. Spoils of influence. Thing
Is. The world must end. Must fascinate such
And such torment to mortgage its dark chase.
Déjenos. Let us go. Buenas noches.

ENEMY OF THE ABSOLUTE

I

Whose attending spirit holds me thus?

Whose shape-shifting wood

Thus tooled what

Kind of stew or meanness so

Sweetest sigh, a sudden face, a cliff that wears my

Own steps in

Darkness hush

Of words be beggarly, be master and native

To the gleaming glade.

II

Bright crowns and hills that wreathe

The innards of the nightingale.

A laugh whose inner bark

Scrapes against the olive leaves, dark green

And gray green, citations of aloha,

Movements of the cross.

From the outside

We are all tormented, jangling our bracelets

From heaven, its rural scent of knowing

What acts are now before us.

III

The Mexico we are still young from
Faking our own deaths
As children, shaking our futures
Before your eyes—
How warm the night is
With these feelings you've been avoiding.
The summer we spent in Oaxaca
Is at the same time inconceivable
And without eternity.

IV

For they teach us that eternity is

Not always where the mind is, nor held in judgment

By its furnishings, a beautiful sunset

Of human spirit.

Humid night.

Hamburger in mind, mind

White towel of imagery.

Weapons that turn outward to connect

With the harmony of things come not now

From the mind.

V

Perfect blue of the galaxy.

Stars that paddle across our eyes, across the yogurt and dream

Of the Persian Gulf

Have no gunmen to the fault.

Nor in the prehensile television of our minds

To retrace what we've killed, playing

Tricks on the dead.

Upward angel

Downward fish.

My face

Alone, and the sky.

NIGHT FALLS

I

也许是不诚实的　Night falls
这一首诗　Night falls

失眠。　一阵　Night falls. This
春风　Disquiet

翻起人群中的幽灵。　白纸中的　Relating to failure. I shake my hair
一棵青墨核桃，一棵　In the hollows

无人理睬的核桃　Of freedom, beginning to end
在海中翻滚　Is freedom.

TRANSLATION

Maybe it is dishonest
This poem

Loss of sleep. A burst
Of spring wind

Stirs ghosts in the crowd. On this white sheet
Of paper is a blue walnut, a

Walnut no one notices
Stirring in sea

II

后来，发现留在记忆中的　Having finally fallen asleep

大大天空　In this other country. For eight months
排除纸上的深意　I have been on holiday.

却相似自己的生命
飘浮在绝对和孤独的崒影上

TRANSLATION

And then, discovering that in one's memory

The large, large sky
Removed from its deeper contents on

Paper is much like your own life, floating above this
Lonely and absolute shadow of one's spit

III

拼命拥抱沙漠里散出的血味　The darkness I wipe now

沙沙的春风　From my nose. Friends I can almost
粘上纸　Call out their names.

石下河水　Life hangs down.
所取笔原形　The branches of memory hang down.

花儿无骨，一笔一笔　It was summer
摸开这不真实的光线　And I could see the reflection of everything.

TRANSLATION

In the desert emitting this blood smell I hug and hug

Whoosh whoosh spring wind
Sticks to paper

A rock slipped in
A river asks the pen to restore it

Flower without bone, stroke after stroke
Rub away this unrealistic light

IV

好亲婆

你变成了一只刺猬！ 从一本很薄的诗
集匆忙地爬了出来。 听我说：

世界上
没有痛苦，没有失落，没有欺骗！ 没有疲倦中的空虚。
在一个森林里，我们赛跑。 我问你

为什么不穿鞋子。 你笑，笑了好长时间。 惊惊！ 你口袋里的黑暗
马上要追上我了！ For as shadows of ourselves appear
As grass upon the grass.

TRANSLATION

Grandmother

You've turned into a hedgehog! From a very thin book
Of poems hurriedly crawling out. Listen to me:

In the world
There is no pain, no loss, no dishonesty! No emptiness from exhaustion.
In a forest, we race. I ask you

Why you are not wearing shoes. You laugh. Laughing for awhile. Lynn! The darkness in your pocket
Is catching up to me

V

Emptiness

As it seemed to me
A long time had passed.

The clutter on one's desk.
As above all is emptiness.

I am sorry I could not keep you in my mind.
I am a bad person.

My heart is so light.

LULLABIES

For what offense

The grave drew near

No crew remembers me

I felt the final inch

Around my feet the sea

No more a child

Did take me for its bride

For Hart Crane

Are these pillars or are these waves

Slicing my cheeks like scuds of wheat

Eyelid by eyelid dividing me

O thou O hear

These thornless stalks of air

There is no time to lose

No keeping more obscene

No do not shout like that

Upon the sunlit limits of the night

Blindly pass

No work of words

Survey the senate of our minds

For Frank O'Hara

Dear Frank. I am writing you a letter with nowhere to send it. We've taken a room in San Felipe, on the Calle de los Claveles. Separating the bedrooms are fifteen paces covering the length of our courtyard. Purple jacarandas seesaw above us and in the street, blouses dissolve like lozenges to release the natural color. At night we are carried out with our noses missing. Darkness spreads from person to person. Black hills outstretch the rugged profile of the soil.

For Federico García Lorca

The moon is an insect the autumn wind

Brushes it away

For Gu Cheng

Autumn 1981

I am not born

But my clothes are blowing in the street

And through the trees

Flowing up along the road

For Emily Dickinson

夜
也
页
野

For Danielle Collobert

One leaf touches another and not as comparison

For Paul Celan

Asylum is a dead man's word brother

It is embarrassing to die to see

The sky below as an abyss and hear

Its horny thrush of frost thread shadows on the sea

The sky so blue upon the water sings

Its grave is green and through me runs the grass

But blindness does not furnish blindness brings

Night down to the blended notes that children in their class-

Rooms sing brother sunset after sunset

Do we not walk through crocuses in bloom?

The dead do walk upon their heads and yet

The headless one emits a bright perfume

God's rainbow do we sing and singing did undress

The serpents that we name brother we are blessed

Whose thoughts are these we clothe

By cadence of,

Margaret, ourselves

In the pageantry of nature's wood?

A child who steps into the air

Braids the congress of its kiss sucking

Lace upon the lily-locks

Unfurls

By what force? Father:

If we weep for fortune, must we also

Take her eyes? The heart peels back

Its crimson soil a wreath

In which time unleaving did

Row back, backward its small current

For Friedrich Hölderlin

Whose face still joins to living

Its furnished smoke? It was

A warring cloak

Grieving wood

A coward

Calling back its chorus

From the caves who hears

Its ancient builders strike our stones?

Whose stony fists whose spears

Falling all around

The angels reappeared

To still the torches' painted path

Upon which our shepherds fled

Backwards and forward

In through time

The double-face of Heaven

Is not a sign

Bend not to my knowledge

For I have divided all of my seasons with you

For Jack Spicer

What shadow

What follows

For whom

Is left?

Angel—

Move your feet!

For Attila József

What rose as vapor now

Turns to weeping a walking

Ghost to still the bells

At labor's end the dregs of

Echo fail

For Miguel Hernández

Bread on the inside bread we cannot eat

Blind to crocodiles blind to wind

Bread soil bread shade bread sun

And there are leaves many leaves branches

That telescope into the brain in my

Country we are uneasy

Because of the light that bread emits

In your country it seems darkness

Cut away

I have split my finger on the geranium. A drop of blood climbs out. I follow it drunk and staggering through the street. Into alleyways among heaps of trash clinging to blue branches as it multiplied. As it sat down on our trains and with our friends a ring of smoke knocks on our door. Our eyes dissolve into the laughter. Into chains of pure flowing hair. Volcanoes undulate. Machines undulate. The wheat on Saturn mixes with the sorrow of our crocodiles. Do you notice anything foreign in me? My suffering has disappeared.

For Osip Mandelstam

By shade of palm-slash

And by blood drying on the wind illusion

And I parted ways

I went to the dogs barking

Like women in the street

I touched them drank from them

They did not notice me

For Marina Tsvetaeva

All season I walk

With his shadow on my face

I sleep with him as with other men

I am indifferent

Laughing when he laughs

Drinking and dancing

One night

Slamming his fist down on our table

He takes me by the throat

Drags me through the street

For Vladimir Mayakovsky

War winding down

Street through our trenches

Strong and naked—

Listen!

If it's any consolation

I'll be dead soon / you can always pay

Somebody the Devil follows

Day and night he is afraid

To be alone / wearing me around

Like a necklace

Sets down his helmet

As I raise my fist—this bug I'd squashed

Now turns to face me in the night

Mother / do you sing?

Don't let us poets fool you—

Our laboratories equipped only

With illusion

Pity us

Fill your eyes with chandeliers

Cross the bridge to join the crowd

For Jules Laforgue

Do you see who spits into your eyes? Their hollow smiles

Hang with sour faces on the wind

Wolf-howl on the alter, their leaning heads, night-effect—

Odilon! I dream of you! Returning from Tahiti I strangle you

I wrestle you from my skull a talisman

I am leaving Europe

Europe! Stinking with carcasses and trades I am slave to

your rooms, your lamplight, the mille-fleur flat silk of wall

I cannot leave you! I am drunk

I am shot in the heart

I am Baudelaire

Rimbaud

I am Odilon

Zip myself into the flower-suit blow smoke into the sky

For Antonin Artaud

I DIE! I DISOBEY! I SHATTER

SO SLOWLY I LOSE CONSCIOUSNESS

Into your volcano your SHADOWMOUTH I drink myself

FALL IN   EAT   TOUCH MY LIFE

PLUNGE A STRAW INTO THE EARTH SUCK OUT YOUR IRISES

Life slips away

Like dust

The blush of childhood squeezes

From our mother tongue

A bullet I had never seen

So jealous so self-pitying   ANTONIN   I HAVE SEEN YOUR BLOOD C A S

C A D I N G F R O M O U R T E M P L E S

I HAVE WALKED INSIDE YOUR DREAMS BEHIND YOUR EYES I STAB

YOU COUNTLESS TIMES   CLIMB ONTO YOUR BALCONY

C R Y O U T I N Y O U R V O I C E

For Charles Baudelaire

Lie me down to heal in sleep, do not let me wake

In sin, the tongue

Cancels another year, another painted storm

In the coral caves, some pious poet

Drunk on vapors

Swatting tomb-bats in the nightwood, would that

Wayward bark sunned white

Be also thunder, a hill of bones drumming—thud

Thud, a wake

Of buzzards braiding into the loosening skull—the redoubled fists

Of students like an island in the bramble chained—I have been told

To reason, lawless, empty, without rights—

But I am old

Not age, I have been told

To match its columns by our footfall, prophet—I am not

The straw or garland of our Sirens, not the brow

Of holly, nor the warble

Of any lark

For John Berryman

Sing warrior songs rain songs sing the Times sing light

Soil stone shade sing rock

Songs

Dream

Songs sing

Isolde

In Tahiti Faust

In Haiti lions dolphins manatees sing

I saw

My friend sing

In the

Abyss his

Singing did not carry me

But followed joint-

By joint see-

Sawing in the breeze and there

I saw him fall

Down he went

Darkness does not come to sing

Tethered

Like a comma to the air

Broods on Henry's shy and spindly nerve

To meet a flower

And suffer when it fails to bloom—O

Jealous worm

Does terror not also

Decorate? Mon frère

Mon frère

Ballad of the air

Who could see you and forget

The blue eye quivering

From its root?

Savage

Smile upon these words and things

And sing for god's sake

Savage

Sing

A

Velvet

Coif of blond

Falls from the bridge of your nose

And the tiny needle on the zodiac

Draws a tinier claw

Pillars of transparent fire the poet lay underneath

Rehearsing to make a grade

At age twenty-eight

The prudential balm

That summer brings

Lacerations in the brain a shrapnel

Of the dark

Smears in night's stride gleams

The eye shakes

From its grave

Gradual self-

Loathing dark

Crumples in our clothes—mon frère

Mon frère

Ballad of the air

DEBTS & LESSONS

Death unburdened nothing

But a tunnel of sunlight

Pinned to lilac

Leaves mindful

Of the sweetening

Itself moving countless

Sunbeams

Fire

Here passeth

Hyacinths

From our eyes spring

Entrails of sky

Face covered in sweet jam

I hid in the palm of a banana flower sick

Squint into the armpit

Not safe

Until tied down

To some sort of money

Not

For the dignity to fail and why

Not? Lest

Nothing tear open

Its cage the liver sang warbles

Of song

Smell

Of shadow moving leaf

To leaf bending downward

Toward the earth gave beauty

To our nothingness O

Fire

Could not stay

And fire could find no syllable no

Common cave to slow

Our blindness which poetry

Then forgave

Returning us to our meadowed paths

The pathless ways where weeping stood

Unclothed and simple

Be our trades

O century of clouds! Ear that shepherds

A little onward

A little further on a thorn

Awakens the intestines

Snaking through the grass awha awha

Awha the lashes

Of wheat awha the spear

Of ash awha

And tubers sinking upward past the grave

The gurgling

Of that mother sound

Awha

I sing it

To the Anamu

To the nettles and the cabbage tree

I sing it to my daughter Piri-

Piri awha

Who sings it to her daughter

Awha and her daughter's daughter's daughter

Feather of the lightning

Amu

Water from the night

Life flows backward into night

Rain sound dropping

Like ants onto the table

We snatch at them with our hands

Ah here! I've got one

It squirms

Into my eye and takes root there

It is wild and it is bitter

To whom am I speaking? From whom

Do I drift? Angel

Of the unmarked path

In you

The eyes of death did move

Like the ruffled edges of a dress

The flint and bone-

Silk of its face

Silver and dark there passed awhile

A fragment

It is not

But ask it

Fills with silence

Do not be embarrassed

We fall against our ghosts

Sometimes

Hear the dolphin sigh

And slink along the muddy banks

One by one by two

A drop of blood dividing

No eyes no nose no ear our tears

Rattle inside their shells

Rain downward

And sideways

Through our chests

Rain between chest

And sky a heap

Of human faces I climbed

Over my children and my children's

Children sunlight

Pours down

Through the leaves

Rustling with borrowed

Skin squatting

There in the gorse

Hair smeared wild

Objectless

Child

I call you back

Under the divisions

Right foot

Left foot

Fingernail

Nightingale

Say river

Who will quench it

Napalm the green-

Eyed grazing flower sulfur

Islets of blue

Hibiscus

Dust

Saliva

Mother

Your smile pulls across

My face I cry out

To feel it

Again all

Things valentine

Of

Mother

Is that you?

Part

River part

Smoke idling sea-

Sick bac

Bac barked

The liana-

Belt silver lima

Lima I

Hollow in the earth have made

Away

Ishfay annot-

Cay idehay ehindbay

O

Swimming upward

Through the crags and rubbled

Bowels of gathering crowd whose voices

Do you hurl

Skyward and whose

In the misty sea-spray now return

New tears into your eyes?

Breath of the old world

Still wearing its slashed throat its spears

And scarves still tangled in undealt wind

A rib of smoke the sky

Sucked in speaking

And weeping

In their shells whose bodies

Do we safeguard

Whose rights in wavy moonlight climbed

And climbed into the high-rise stabbing shooting raiding hammering

Onto our streets in uniform

Sewers of putrefaction

Of spirit of acacia wild of pillage

Of spears of wheat and hammock

Intestines fulgent unwaking

Mirror of thunder time

Sweetens swale

Of shrub and ash

Of passage door to door a wave

Of torches of linen of restless

Labor of twilight fire devoured

In vain

I jab the spurs of desire into its side

Ask me again

That parted our estate

Ask me

From the soil

Of self-contempt the wilderness

Of conflicting counsel ask me

Fata

Morgana shelled

Worm of sea

Whose effervescent reefs

Bent into arcades and above us

Rose the aqueducts

Of ancient Rome

Billow of vomit

Graves

If graves they were

A wingspan of time

An axe

A serpent

Soft and restless will with war

Heart harden

And rose-flush

To its cheeks restore

A senate

A walking word

Hurrying back into the fire

The lullaby for Emily Dickinson plays with one sound. In Mandarin all four characters have the phonetic translation of "ye" and moves within two tonal registers. Amongst others, yè also carries the sound for *leaf* (or *leaves*) and for the word *industry*.

yè	yě	yè	yě
夜	也	页	野
Night	Also	Pages	Wild

ACKNOWLEDGMENTS

Thank you to my parents Hai Liu and Chengyi Xu. My husband Joshua Edwards. My teachers Charles Altieri, Jim Barnabee, Forrest Gander, Robert Hass, Lyn Hejinian, Geoffrey G. O'Brien, Keith Waldrop, Rosmarie Waldrop and C.D. Wright. My friends Noam Biale, Michael Tod Edgerton, Layla Nova Forrest-White, Jane Gregory, Louis Gropman, Anna Hankow, Aaron Lammer, Andrew Moisey, Sawako Nakayasu, Ariel Perloff, Katie Peterson, Dalia Rinaldi, Jessica Sato, Kate Schapira, Kendra Sullivan, Bronwen Tate, Michelle Ty and Caroline Noble Whitbeck.

Thank you Anne Carson and Phoebe for selecting *Say You Will Die for Me* for the 2006 Greg Grummer Award; Charles Wright for including it in the 2008 Best American Poetry anthology; Octopus, Tinfish and Zoland Poetry for publishing earlier versions of *Earth Light* and *Enemy of the Absolute*; Ben Lerner and Boston Review for featuring parts of *Lullabies* and *Night Falls* in the Poet's Sampler; Critical Quarterly and CLOCK for printing more *Lullabies*; Fanny Howe and SLS for inviting me to St. Petersburg in 2007; U.S. Fulbright Program and the Jacob. K. Javits Fellowship Program; Rusty Morrison, Ken Keegan and Cassandra Smith.

You are what make this book.

Lynn Xu was born in Shanghai. Her poems have appeared in *6x6, 1913, Best American Poetry 2008, Boston Review, Octopus, Poor Claudia,* and others. A chapbook, *June,* was published by Corollary Press in 2006. The recipient of a Fulbright Fellowship and a William L. Magistretti Fellowship, she is currently the Jacob K. Javits Fellow at UC Berkeley, where she is a Ph.D. candidate in Comparative Literature. She holds an MFA from Brown University. With Robyn Schiff, Nick Twemlow, and husband Joshua Edwards, she coedits Canarium Books. Between Stuttgart and Marfa, she divides her time.

Debts & Lessons
by Lynn Xu

Cover text set in Gil Sans Std
Interior text set in Perpetua Std

Cover art by Lynn Xu
"Study of Rousseau," 2012.

Cover design by Joshua Edwards
Interior layout by Cassandra Smith

Omnidawn Publishing
Richmond, California
2013

Ken Keegan & Rusty Morrison, Co-Publishers & Senior Editors
Cassandra Smith, Poetry Editor & Book Designer
Gillian Hamel, Poetry Editor & OmniVerse Managing Editor
Sara Mumolo, Poetry Editor
Peter Burghardt, Poetry Editor & Book Designer
Turner Canty, Poetry Editor
Juliana Paslay, Fiction Editor & Bookstore Outreach Manager
Liza Flum, Poetry Editor & Social Media
Sharon Osmond, Poetry Editor & Bookstore Outreach
Gail Aronson, Fiction Editor
RJ Ingram, Social Media
Craig Santos Perez, Media Consultant